Plumbing Guide

320 Extremely Useful Plumbing Tips Every Home Owner Should Know

By Adam Gold

Published by Liraz Publishing

www.bizmove.com

320 Extremely Useful Plumbing Tips Every Home Owner Should Know

Unfortunately, most homeowners find that plumbing issues tend to rear their head soon after a new property is purchased. The majority of the time this happens in the kitchen or bathroom. In reality, at some point each homeowner deals with a plumbing problem at some point. This book will provide you with all the knowledge you need to tackle any plumbing problems.

Please note that a few of the tips in this book repeat themselves. It is done intentionally as research shows that this may help you better remember the advice provided in this book.

Tips start here:

Some people have problems with their plumbing system in that the pipes sweat and drip condensation. You do not have to hire a plumber to take care of this nuisance. You can purchase self-adhesive drip tape from your local hardware store. This drip tape will insulate your "sweating" pipes which are dripping with moisture built up from condensation. To make sure the tape sticks firmly, dry the pipe thoroughly before applying the tape.

In order to keep your garbage disposal in optimal working condition, run it on a regular basis. Just a simple 60 seconds per day under cold water can keep it running clean and smooth. If not run regularly, your disposal can be susceptible to corrosion that will eventually make it inoperable.

One way to prevent pipes from freezing during the winter is to keep cabinet doors in your house that contain the pipes open. This can insure that they get adequate heat to keep warm. Make sure also, to unhook and kind of hose outside and run a little water to clear the pipes of any remaining water going outside.

Don't start any do-it-yourself plumbing project without having a plan in place. You need to know beforehand exactly what you are getting yourself into. Know what kind of space you are working with and what lines are which. Getting a clear picture early on will make your plumbing project go a lot smoother!

Frozen pipes can cause a lot of damage and cost you money. However, this can typically be prevented. Make sure that any outdoor pipes are well insulated. Also, when it starts to get colder, drain and disconnect your hoses and turn off the outside faucet. Doing so can prevent some nasty repair bills a professional plumber would charge you.

If you have an odor coming from one or more fixtures in your house, it is likely this has to do with the water in water traps. Each fixture has a water trap that is sealed off to prevent odors. If the water evaporates, the odors can surface. Therefore, try adding water to the traps.

Have a specific plumber in mind before you have an emergency. Most people don't think about plumbers until they find themselves having a big problem that needs to be fixed right away. Instead, choose a plumber who you are comfortable with and whose experience you trust--way before you actually need his services.

The key to finding a great plumber for new construction is to look at their prior jobs. Good plumbers take pride in the work they do, so they will have photos and references from previous jobs. If the plumber you are considering hiring does not have references or photos of previous jobs, then stay away and find another.

Many people complain of low water pressure. While there are several things that can cause this, one must not be overlooked when starting your investigation. What kind of pipes do you have? If your piping is galvanized, you are better off just replacing your piping which will eliminate the issue.

To compare the quality of your pipes or sewers over time, create a video for documentation purposes. Several months later, make the same video so that you can see if there are any new cracks or holes that require fixing. This can serve as a great way to analyze your infrastructure.

Clean washing machine lint traps and use pantyhose over the water outlet tube to prevent lint, fuzz and other debris from clogging sewer or septic system filters. Fine mesh traps are also available for this purpose, but a package of knee-high nylon stockings and plastic ties can provide enough filters to encourage you to do the job regularly.

To prepare for the cold weather, properly drain all outside faucet bibs and turn off the water supply to those faucets. A piece of foam taped to the outside bib can provide excellent insulation to prevent any remaining water from freezing or splurge for a specialty cover that comes complete with Velcro closures.

You should consider getting a stainless steel sink if you are in need of a new sink. Stainless steel sinks are much better than other ones for many reasons. They are more durable, they absorb shock, they are easier to clean, and they go with almost any decor.

If you must call a professional to repair your plumbing problem, be prepared with a list of all of your plumbing problems, no matter how small or trivial. Plumbers typically charge a set fee just to make a house call, usually the price of one hour of their time. But, if they can fix your initial problem in a few minutes, you will get more value for that service call and avoid having to pay for another, by having them check out other issues.

If you need to get a new toilet, be sure you go with a trustworthy brand. Cheap toilets are more likely to break down easily and you will end up having to buy a new one. If you are unsure of which brands are good, ask the salesperson in a home improvement store.

Do not put cooking oils, fat, or grease, down your drain. These fats cause clogs by solidifying in pipes.

To properly dispose of fats, put them in a bowl with a lid that you can dispose of. Once it gets hard, throw it in the trash or compost bin.

Check your gas water heater periodically to make sure the pilot flame is lit. The correct color for this flame should be blue. The tip of the flame should be yellow. If you find that you are only seeing a yellow flame, you may need to call a professional for safety reasons.

If you notice orange or pink stains in your bathroom fixtures, this is because of the iron in your water. Water softener can help this problem, and you can buy that at a store. Alternatively, you can hire someone to handle it.

DIY plumbing jobs will require that you understand how to solder copper for the lines for the water supply. You can practice this skill so that you will be able to run your lines without worrying about it leaking. Search online for video tutorials that can help you get a handle on how to go about soldering.

Do not, under any circumstances, put lemons down your disposal. Although the lemon smell will give your disposal a great smell, its acid can corrode the metal parts in it. Instead, use products that are made specifically for this use. You can purchase these products at most hardware stores or wherever cleaning products are sold.

Before embarking on a plumbing project, make sure that you're aware of where the shutoff valve for water in your home is, as well as the valves for shutting off individual structures like sinks, toilets, etc. This way, if something goes wrong, you'll be able to stop the water flow.

You have no choice in the matter of what plumber is scheduled sometimes, but you should still research different plumbers online. Even if your insurance provider has assigned you someone of their choosing, find out who it is online and check do a web search for ratings of previous customers, so that you can be prepared for their arrival.

In any DIY plumbing project, make sure that you always test the drains and the supply lines before you close up the walls. It is a lot easier to find and solve problems if you look for them while you are still in the process of actively doing the job.

To help you find a good plumber, you should get recommendations from people whom you trust. Asking a friend or a neighbor is usually more trustworthy than picking a random plumber out of the phone book. You need a competent plumber; otherwise you could be in for a much bigger problem down the road.

During the warm seasons, you will see that there will be many bird nests forming in and around your plumbing vent pipes. It is essential to clear these out, as they can have a devastating effect on the quality of your plumbing and the flow of water in your home.

In the winter months, if you live somewhere where temperatures fall below freezing, leave your faucets on a little bit to let a thin stream of water through. This will help prevent the pipes from freezing, which could be a major problem for you and all the pipes in your home.

When searching for a good plumber you should always check references. It is easy to just go with the lowest price, but you have to do your research and make sure the plumber has a good reputation with the people they have done work for in the past so you do not get a bad plumber.

During the week, hair and soap can build up in your drains and can cause serious clogs. Make sure that you have strainers in each of your drains to help catch this debris so that it does not become an issue. This will help to keep your water flowing efficiently.

Consult your Department of Consumer Affair if you're looking to hire a plumbing contractor. You can learn if a contractor's license is valid and if any complaints have been filed against them. If a plumber does not have a current license and even a limited number of complaints, you probably don't want them working on your home.

Check for leaks behind the wall tile in your bathroom, especially any tile surrounding your bathtub, by gently pressing each tile and feeling for some give. If you find any mushy or soft spots, you will need to find the source of the leak and repair it to prevent further damage.

A great way to save a few dollars is to add insulation to your hot water heater. Much of the energy required to heat the water in your home is the expense from keeping the water in the tank hot for when it is needed. Adding an extra layer of insulation can help reduce this cost.

To clear mineral deposits from your showerhead,

try a soak in white vinegar. Simply add a cup or two of vinegar to a plastic bag and tape it around the showerhead, ensuring that it is submerged. Leave the bag on for an hour, and the vinegar will dissolve the mineral build-up, allowing water to gush through like it was when it was new.

It is imperative as a homeowner that you know exactly where your main water shut-off valve is located and can operate the valve in case of an emergency. The best first step measure for frozen pipes is to stop water from entering your home in the first place. Locate the main water supply valve and turn it on and off on a regular basis to keep it easily operable in an emergency.

Roots from a tree in your back yard can be a real headache when it comes to plumbing. Make sure if you have a big tree or bush or some kind of plant with a big root system, that you ask your plumbing company about root killing agents. You can flush these down your toilet and kill any roots that may be blocking your pipes and save yourself a lot of money by stopping a back up before it happens.

Make sure everyone that lives in your house knows where to find and use the main water shut off valve in case there is a burst pipe emergency. This is especially important if you live in an area where your pipes may freeze. Take a moment to show your family members where the valve is and how to properly shut it off.

Do not put cooking oils, fat, or grease, down your drain. These fats cause clogs by solidifying in pipes. To properly dispose of fats, put them in a bowl with a lid that you can dispose of. Once it gets hard, throw it in the trash or compost bin.

Unclog drains with ease. Try using a plunger and drain cleaner, as your clog may simply be a build-up of hair and debris. If this doesn't work you may have to clear the drain with a snake. Feed the snake into the drain line as far as it will go. Turn the crank gently, which will help to loosen the clog. Remove the snake, and run water down the drain to see if the clog has been removed. You may have to use the snake a couple of times, before the clog is cleared so don't give up!

Always buy a high quality fixture if you are going to replace your shower head. Sometimes, people will choose a shower head because it is the least expensive. Usually these break easily.

If your toilet is constantly developing moisture on the outside, you may want to consider turning up the heat in your bathroom. The biggest cause of "sweaty" toilets is cool and moist air. Believe it or not, this moisture could actually cause damage to your toilet, so it is crucial that you fix the problem.

Is your toilet leaking? Find out by putting some food color in the tank and then check the bowl later. If there is colored water in the bowl, the toilet has an internal leak. To fix an internal leak you can simply replace the tank's ball or flapper.

If water is backing up into multiple fixtures all over the house, it is no longer going to be effective for you to use chemicals or a small hand snake. This is evidence of a blockage in the main line, and you must contact a professional to take care of this problem for you.

One way to prevent water heater problems is to turn down the heat. As long as the water is still as hot as needed for showers and washing dishes, turning it down won't hurt anything, and will extend the life of the heater. Holding very hot water can corrode the inside.

In the winter months, if you live somewhere where

temperatures fall below freezing, leave your faucets on a little bit to let a thin stream of water through. This will help prevent the pipes from freezing, which could be a major problem for you and all the pipes in your home.

To keep the pipes in your kitchen in tip-top shape, avoid pouring fats or cooking oils down the drain. These liquid fats solidify in the pipes and create clogs. As an added protection, wipe congealed grease from pots to further avoid creating clogged drains. By following these tips, you can help avoid a plumbing disaster.

Hair can clog your drains if you do not clean them regularly. You could also get some screens to place over your drains to keep most of the hair from going down. Hair usually breaks down, but it can cause your drains to back up if they are present in large quantity.

If you cannot turn off your main water valve before leaving on vacation, turn off the individual valves for the toilets, sinks, and washing machine. If the valves do not look like they are in good working order, then leave them on and that will be something that you need to have changed when you return.

To avoid hair from accumulating and clogging pipes. Use fine mesh strainers in every drain where hair is washed. Fine mesh strainers can catch the hair and still allow the shower, tub or sink to drain and are also useful in the kitchen to catch and stop small food debris from going down the drain.

If you are the kind of person who likes to listen to music when you work, then you should be sure to avoid using headphones. A radio is a much smarter choice, as it will allow you to hear the music you want, without distracting you from hearing important sounds.

If you absolutely need to contact a plumber, be careful with the professional that you pick. Like mechanics, plumbers are experts in their particular field, and they may try to convince you to do a job or service that is completely unnecessary given your problem. Try to find one who has gotten good reviews, especially when it comes to honesty.

Rigid copper is used for main water lines in many homes. You cannot bend rigid copper, so joints and tees must be soldered on. When soldering, always apply flux (also called soldering paste) to both surfaces. Flux retards oxidation when the copper is heated. Always use lead-free or nearly lead-free solder when sweating a copper joint.

Check the filters in your furnace, regularly. If these filters have not been cleaned or replaced recently, they may become clogged. This will affect how well your furnace is able to work, meaning that you may not have enough heat during the winter. Take this simple step, as soon as the weather starts to become cold.

On very cold winter nights, allow your faucets to trickle slightly, especially if your pipes are located in a crawlspace. The running water prevents the pipes from freezing as quickly as they would otherwise. You can catch the water and use it for other household needs to prevent wasting it.

Make sure you know where your home's water shutoff is located. You never know when there might be an emergency involving a broken pipe or damaged connection that requires you to turn off the water right away. In addition, knowing where the shutoff is located is vital before you start any plumbing project, in case anything goes wrong.

Don't use harsh chemicals such as toilet tablets in

your toilet. They can clean the bowl and remove odors, but they also damage the soft plastic and rubber parts in and around your toilet.

Do not put your hand in the garbage disposal to remove a clog. This can be potentially harmful. Always use tongs to get out whatever is stuck in the disposal. Using tongs is much safer, and you will make sure your hand does not get cut on the disposer's sharp blades.

Everyone in your home should know where the main water shut off valve is. By knowing where to find this valve, you'll be able to shut off the water in the event a pipe bursts, a bathtub or toilet overflows or any other emergency that requires you to turn off the water.

Regular maintenance of your plumbing lines is a great idea. Your options are getting your lines snaked or jetted. Jetted is a technology that is proven more effective than snaking is. It gets deeper and cleans harder. So jetting is a good idea next time you are having maintenance performed on your lines.

If a plug needs to be removed, there are a few methods you can use. The first method involves a hammer and chisel to loosen the fitting. Your other option to try is to chisel through the out plug.

If your toilet has sewage back-up, then there is a block somewhere along the branch line that connects the sewage and main lines. If you are unable to fix the blockage, you will need to hire a professional to run a snake in the line to clean it.

Before hiring a contractor for plumbing or other jobs, make sure you look into their records through the Department of Consumer Affairs. You can learn if a contractor's license is valid and if any complaints have been filed against them. Do not hire a plumber with a license that is not in good standing.

When looking for a plumber, you have quite a few options. Ask friends for recommendations of who they use. Check online for plumbers with good reviews and references. Use your yellow pages and look under "Plumbing Contractors" or "Plumbing, Drain and Sewer Cleaning". Make sure that you contact more than one plumber before making a choice.

Make sure you shut off your main system before leaving your house for a few weeks. The water will stay in the pipes, but this should prevent any further damages in case a leak starts while you are away. Check that your shut-off valve is working properly before you leave.

Protect you plumbing pipes! If you live in an area which has cold winters and are leaving your home for an extended amount of time, protect your plumbing while you are gone! Shut off the main water valve! Drain the system of water by opening the faucets at the highest and lowest points of the house. Also, make sure that you have left some heat on in the house! Set the thermostat to at least 55 degrees Fahrenheit.

Do not pour grease and oil down your drains. Cooking grease will build up in your pipes and could cause back-ups. Keep grease and oil in a container in your fridge and throw it in the trash when it is full. Avoid clogging your pipes with any products containing oil or grease.

When you are working with plumbing, you also need to have some basic skills in other areas. This is especially true of electrical problems, as the two systems often overlap. This doesn't mean that you need to solve the problems, but that you understand what the problems could be.

A great plumbing tip which can save you a lot of money on a daily basis is to invest in a low GPF (gallons per flush) model toilet. As such, every time you flush the toilet you will be using less water than before, and doing so will save you on your water bill.

Always try plunging any clogged toilet or drain before snaking. Snaking can often push problems further down the pipe and make matters worse. A plunger uses nothing but your strength and water pressure to help clear clogs. For more effective plunging, boil some water and pour into the affected drain or toilet to help loosen things up before plunging.

Before you start a plumbing project you should tighten all of the pipes that are easily accessible. Especially if your pipes are making a range of loud banging sounds, as this is a clear sign that there are loose pipes along the line. It is also a good idea in case there is a clog so the excess pressure released does not break a loose pipe.

If you have bad water pressure in the shower, the showerhead might be clogged. Take a plastic baggie, fill it with regular vinegar, and tie it to the showerhead so that the showerhead is covered. Leave it overnight. In the morning, take the baggie off and use a small toothbrush to scrub away any mineral deposits.

Use a strainer over your sink drain to catch food and other bits of material. Otherwise, you will likely get a clogged drain. You should clean your strainer in your kitchen anytime you have anything in it. You should clean out the strainer in your bathtub often.

A great way to knock out your plumbing issues in one shot is to schedule everything at once. You might be tempted to call the plumber every time you need something fixed, but if you wait and hire the plumber for a single visit, you can save up money for repairs. It also saves you money because a lot of plumbers charge by the hour--they cannot charge for multiple hours every trip if they only make one trip out.

Find out the plumbing codes in your local area before starting any project. Plumbing codes can vary wildly from area to area and you don't want to run afoul of the codes. Visit your local building department to find out information or hire a plumber for a day to help you go over your plans and provide advice.

DIY plumbing jobs will require that you understand how to solder copper for the lines for the water supply. You can practice this skill so that you will be able to run your lines without worrying about it leaking. Search online for video tutorials that can help you get a handle on how to go about soldering.

There are two ways to remove clean out plugs. First, you can hammer a chisel around the fitting base to loosen it. The only other alternative is to chisel through the plug.

In any DIY plumbing project, make sure that you always test the drains and the supply lines before you close up the walls. It is a lot easier to find and solve problems if you look for them while you are still in the process of actively doing the job.

If water is flooding your home, immediately switch off the main electrical power. If water comes into contact with any electrical components, it can become a fatal situation. Once the power is off, then deal with the flood water. Put your own and your family's personal safety first, and show each member of the family how to shut off the power.

If the pipes have burst in an upstairs area, use a tool to perforate the ceiling underneath in several places and places pots and pans under to catch the water. If this is not done, the weight of the accumulating water could cause a collapse of the entire ceiling.

Do not pour grease and oil down your drains. Cooking grease will build up in your pipes and could cause back-ups. Keep grease and oil in a container in your fridge and throw it in the trash when it is full. Avoid clogging your pipes with any products containing oil or grease.

To compare the quality of your pipes or sewers over time, create a video for documentation purposes. Several months later, make the same video so that you can see if there are any new cracks or holes that require fixing. This can serve as a great way to analyze your infrastructure.

Use a pipe snake if your washing machine drain stack overflows. Lint can build up in the washing machine and cause a clog, which will lead to overflowing.

One of the most inexpensive plumbing issues is a

running toilet. Simply by understanding how a toilet actually functions is the first best tool in avoiding a running toilet. If you understand the function of the lever and floater, you will be able to fix any running toilet in no time.

If you are the kind of person who likes to listen to music when you work, then you should be sure to avoid using headphones. A radio is a much smarter choice, as it will allow you to hear the music you want, without distracting you from hearing important sounds.

Never pour grease of any kind down your kitchen drains, especially grease from animal sources, which tends to harden rather quickly. The grease can congeal in your pipes and cause disastrous clogs and back-ups. It's better to dispose of grease in the trash to keep your drains flowing well.

If you must call a professional to repair your plumbing problem, be prepared with a list of all of your plumbing problems, no matter how small or trivial. Plumbers typically charge a set fee just to make a house call, usually the price of one hour of their time. But, if they can fix your initial problem in a few minutes, you will get more value for that service call and avoid having to pay for another, by having them check out other issues.

Avoid the bursting of pipes due to the change in the temperature. You need to allow the flow of heat to reach under the sinks and into the pipes, you have to keep the cabinet doors of the bathrooms and kitchens open. It is important to keep water running at both hot and cold faucets along with vanities that are in close proximity to exterior walls.

Group all of your plumbing repairs before scheduling a plumber to come out. Check all of your fixtures and faucets. If anything is dripping, running or clogged, make a list for the plumber. That way, when the plumber comes, they can do all of the jobs in one visit. This will cut down on charges.

Watch how your toilets are flushing. If you have to jiggle the handle or if it takes too long, you might have to repair some toilet parts. Replacing these parts early may help you to save on your water bills and will save you from more expensive repairs at a later date.

If you have unwanted water that drains in your dishwasher, it's probably due to the kitchen sink's hose being improperly installed. The hose connecting the kitchen sink and the dishwasher has to go up and then down in order for the water of both locations to not mix.

Some people have problems with their plumbing system in that the pipes sweat and drip condensation. You do not have to hire a plumber to take care of this nuisance. You can purchase self-adhesive drip tape from your local hardware store. This drip tape will insulate your "sweating" pipes which are dripping with moisture built up from condensation. To make sure the tape sticks firmly, dry the pipe thoroughly before applying the tape.

One of the things that you can do to maximize the security of your home is to seal all of the cracks in your outdoor faucets. Even a tiny crack can intensify as the season progresses and lead to serious problems down the road. Reduce drips and leaks for optimal protection.

Don't turn on your sink while using your garbage disposal. It is assumed that food will go down more smoothly if the water is running, though in reality that does nothing good. In contrast, it could actually cause garbage or waste to stick to the insides of the disposal and do more damage than good.

If you have a lot of hair in your shower drain, be sure to get a stopper and put it in the drain. This will catch the hair from going down the drain, which can clog it. Just make sure that you remove hair that is already in the drain before using the stopper.

Make sure you shut off your main system before leaving your house for a few weeks. The water will stay in the pipes, but this should prevent any further damages in case a leak starts while you are away. Check that your shut-off valve is working properly before you leave.

If the water is not going into your dishwasher, the first thing you should do is shit off the water under the sink. Chances are that you have some kind of blockage, and keeping the water turned on could actually create a bigger problem. To fix the blockage, you may need to call a plumber.

When you are going to do laundry in your home washing machine, do not use excess detergent, bleach or other chemicals. Too many of these products can cause the natural bacteria in your septic system to be killed. Just use enough of these products in order to get your laundry done.

Insulate your pipes properly. If the temperature drops below fifty five degrees, your pipes could freeze. This makes pipes extremely fragile and increases the risk of leaks and damages. The pipes inside your house should not freeze but take a look at a plan of your plumbing system to see if you have any pipes outside of your house.

Avoid flushing cotton balls, cotton swabs and any feminine sanitary products down the toilet. Even small panty liners can cause big problems because their adhesive backing can stick to pipes and cause stoppages. Keep a small, covered wastebasket next to the toilet to encourage guests to properly dispose of used sanitary articles.

As tempting as it may be to try and save on the heating bill, keep your furnace set no lower than 55 degrees over the winter to prevent inside pipes from freezing. If you have pipes located in an excessively cold basement, consider running a space heater in the basement, but only when it can be checked on frequently.

A great plumbing tip which can save you a lot of money on a daily basis is to invest in a low GPF (gallons per flush) model toilet. As such, every time you flush the toilet you will be using less water than before, and doing so will save you on your water bill.

Mold growing at the base of your toilet can indicate that condensation is forming on your toilet bowl thanks to room temperature versus bowl and water temperature, or that you have a leak in the wax seal around your toilet. To replace the wax seal, turn off the water to the toilet, disconnect from the water supply and then lift the toilet and replace the ring. The real trick is setting the toilet back down on the ring correctly. Buy an extra ring in case you mess up and to avoid having to run to the hardware store in the middle of the job.

Avoid plumbing problems! Do not stop up the toilet! Some common items that will stop up a toilet include: toys, hair, paper towels, birth control items, and feminine personal products. Do not flush these items down your toilet - unless the instructions say otherwise! These can stop up your toilet - to the point that nothing else will work - except calling a plumber!

Rigid copper is used for main water lines in many

homes. You cannot bend rigid copper, so joints and tees must be soldered on. When soldering, always apply flux (also called soldering paste) to both surfaces. Flux retards oxidation when the copper is heated. Always use lead-free or nearly lead-free solder when sweating a copper joint.

When concerned with plumbing, you need to know what can cause noisy pipes. This is important because it can mean the difference between an annoying noise and flooding in your house. Do your research to distinguish between the different noises and hire a professional if any serious risk is posed.

Use strainers in all drains to catch hair and other objects. This will prevent all the material from going down the drain and causing a clog, which can cause a bigger problem down the line. Clean out the strainers daily so that you don't start getting backup of water in your sink or tub.

Some people have problems with their plumbing system in that the pipes sweat and drip condensation. You do not have to hire a plumber to take care of this nuisance. You can purchase self-adhesive drip tape from your local hardware store.

This drip tape will insulate your "sweating" pipes which are dripping with moisture built up from condensation. To make sure the tape sticks firmly, dry the pipe thoroughly before applying the tape.

One way to prevent pipes from freezing during the winter is to keep cabinet doors in your house that contain the pipes open. This can insure that they get adequate heat to keep warm. Make sure also, to unhook and kind of hose outside and run a little water to clear the pipes of any remaining water going outside.

If your sewer is backed up, there are things you can do to troubleshoot and clean, including renting equipment like a main line cable. However, often times this does not fully take care of the problem. A professional needs to assess the issue then, using a camera method, and thoroughly cleaning the main line.

When you're going away on a vacation, you should consider shutting off the water supply to your home. This can help stop many problems before they start. If you don't do this, you should have someone stop by your house regularly to check that nothing has gone wrong and that your home isn't flooded.

Using a snake tool to remove blockages is very easy. Just insert the tool a few inches into the drain, and then turn the handle to change the direction of the snake head and search for blockages. Continue moving down slowly and searching until you find the cause of your blockage.

When plunging a drain to attempt to remove a blockage, first make sure that the drain is completely covered in water. This helps to form a seal. Then, plunge at least fifteen to twenty times before stopping. Repeat the process two to three times. If this doesn't work, try a chemical drain cleaner.

Valves that are rarely used tend to fuse together. Maintain them with penetrating oil, and rotate them every so often so they don't stick.

Plumbing should only be done by professionals if there is a major problem or if you do not understand plumbing. Many of the big problems that plumbers deal with, actually have simple solutions. The average person, who does not understand the intricacies of plumbing, usually end up compounding the problem by causing other costly damage to the house during the failed repair. The plumber will need to be called in the end, anyway.

Protect you plumbing pipes! If you live in an area which has cold winters and are leaving your home for an extended amount of time, protect your plumbing while you are gone! Shut off the main water valve! Drain the system of water by opening the faucets at the highest and lowest points of the house. Also, make sure that you have left some heat on in the house! Set the thermostat to at least 55 degrees Fahrenheit.

When leaving on vacation or leaving your vacation home, be sure to turn off the main water before you leave. If something happens while you are gone you can cause some serious damage from a flooded basement or a broken pipe in the wall that leaks for weeks until you return.

Do not pour grease and oil down your drains. Cooking grease will build up in your pipes and could cause back-ups. Keep grease and oil in a container in your fridge and throw it in the trash when it is full. Avoid clogging your pipes with any products containing oil or grease.

When installing a brand new water heater, if you see a pipe from the drainage pipe, reconnect it. It's probably a pipe for recirculation, and that does a tremendous job of keeping your water hot without wasting water along the way.

Avoid over-tightening water faucet handles. Use only enough pressure to stop the water from flowing and dripping from the faucet. Anything else is overkill and will quickly wear out the gaskets and washers inside those handles and cause leaking or the inability to stop the water from coming out of the faucet.

To prevent pipes in your house from freezing, do not let the temperature in the house dip below freezing. Also, any pipes exposed to the cold should be insulated. If the temperature surrounding the pipes is anywhere below freezing, this can cause the pipes to freeze. If they do freeze, you are looking at some time before they can thaw out, thus you will have to wait for running water. But, they could also burst, causing a mess and a large repair bill.

Ensure that everyone in your household knows how to turn off the main water supply, or knows how to contact someone who can. In the event of a burst pipe or other water-related emergency, you should immediately turn off the water to prevent flooding, structural damage, and a sky-high water bill.

Only pay the plumber once the job is done. There might be a down payment required, but you do not give him the total cost before he is finished. It is good to know that the plumber did everything as promised before he gets his money.

Use your garbage disposal with the cold water running so that you can preserve the blades of the disposal. Using hot water makes grease more liquid and can cause problems, including clogs. Make sure to clean blades by putting in a little dish detergent and run cold water at the same time.

Taking preemptive action to fix a strange smelling kitchen sink can be a good way to keep your kitchen smelling great. Make sure not to throw hair or grease into your sink. Use baking soda if you have a strange smell coming from your drain. Make sure you use your garbage disposal if you have one to grind up any food and use water while doing this to prevent damage to the blades of the garbage disposal.

Do not overload your garbage disposal. If you need

to dispose of large items, cut them up into smaller pieces. Also, do not put too much in at a time, put one or two items in and wait a few seconds to dispose of the rest. Overloading your disposal can cause the engine to overheat.

If your plumbing is making strange noises you may have lost something called your "air cushion". To turn this back on, you're going to need to turn off your main water supply. Run all faucets in your house and then turn back on your main water supply. This should make everything sound better again.

If your toilet is constantly developing moisture on the outside, you may want to consider turning up the heat in your bathroom. The biggest cause of "sweaty" toilets is cool and moist air. Believe it or not, this moisture could actually cause damage to your toilet, so it is crucial that you fix the problem.

Have your pipes in your plumbing system frozen? You can skip the cost of hiring a plumber by using this method. First, open the faucet so steam produced by the thawing process can escape. Begin thawing close to the faucet, and move down the line as each section thaws out. Use a hair dryer or a heat lamp to warm along the pipe. Even though this method consumes quite a bit of time, it is safer than most other heating methods. Furthermore, it requires no cleanup.

When chilly weather approaches, it is time to disconnect your water hoses from your outside faucets. If you forget to do this, water in the hoses can freeze and expand. This can cause the faucets and the connecting pipes inside your house to freeze and break. By simply rolling up your garden hoses and storing them for the winter, you can help prevent costly plumbing repairs.

When plunging a drain to attempt to remove a blockage, first make sure that the drain is completely covered in water. This helps to form a seal. Then, plunge at least fifteen to twenty times before stopping. Repeat the process two to three times. If this doesn't work, try a chemical drain cleaner.

Keep an eye on your monthly water bill to catch plumbing problems. Has your water bill gone up recently, even though nothing's changed? This could indicate a water leak or appliance problem somewhere inside or outside of your home. Check under sinks for rusted pipes, look for water puddles under outside faucets, and consider having a plumber come out to listen to your pipes to detect running water.

If water is flowing out from where your meter is located, a professional is required to come out and fix the leak. If your water bill goes up, this is most likely because the leak is on the house side of the water meter. You will need to get a professional to come out and fix the leak.

Never try to undertake a project that you are unsure of. Additionally, never call on a friend to help you with something, if they are not a professoinal. There have been hundreds of good friendships ruined by a guy claiming to know exactly what he is doing, when the truth is he is clueless.

To prevent the most common kitchen sink clogs, avoid putting any sort of solid foods down your drain. Many foods, such as eggs and vegetable and fruit waste actually harden with exposure to cold water and over time can form clogs that are next to impossible to remove without professional help.

Plumbing is actually a serious thing, and when you know what the issues are and how to deal with them, you are that much closer to fixing them. Keep these tips on hand while you tackle your plumbing project. Whether you decide to do-it-yourself or call for professional intervention, they will help you gain a better understanding of the situation. Educating yourself is the key to a successful outcome. Plumbing Tips That Can Save You A Bundle

Deciding to become a plumber is a solid career choice. You can work in a variety of settings, including residential and business construction, industrial and residential maintenance and repair and water treatment plants. Here are some tips to help you along.

Rigid copper is used for main water lines in many homes. You cannot bend rigid copper, so joints and tees must be soldered on. When soldering, always apply flux (also called soldering paste) to both surfaces. Flux retards oxidation when the copper is heated. Always use lead-free or nearly lead-free solder when sweating a copper joint.

As the weather begins to get cold, attend to all of your exposed pipes by adding insulation to them. Pay particular attention to pipes located in crawl spaces and the outside walls of your residence. Taking this step will help ensure that your pipes continue to function throughout the winter.

One of the things that you can do to safeguard your home from any serious plumbing issues is to install a flood alarm. This is a device that will sound when it comes in contact with water, alerting you if there are any issues in a particular area in the house.

To be successful in any plumbing project, make sure you turn the water off before you start unscrewing pipes. This tip might actually sound insulting, but you are probably getting caught up in having the right tools and parts and being dressed right. Double check that there is not a splash waiting for you. Then triple and quadruple check.

Believe it or not, it is not a very good idea to use a plunger if your toilet is clogged. Plungers just push whatever is stuck deeper into the drain. Instead, it is a better idea to use a closet auger. It will do a better job and is affordable.

If you have an odor coming from one or more fixtures in your house, it is likely this has to do with the water in water traps. Each fixture has a water trap that is sealed off to prevent odors. If the water evaporates, the odors can surface. Therefore, try adding water to the traps.

When winter is on the horizon, it is particularly important to check your outside water fixtures to ensure they aren't leaking or dripping. If there are drips or leaks, then the repairs need to be done prior to any freezing temperatures. Freezing water can cause pressure to build up, causing your pipes to crack, or burst, regardless if your pipes are constructed with steel, plastic, or metal. One small crack is all it takes to cause serious water damage to your home.

If you have a crack in your toilet tank, you can sometimes fix this with an epoxy resin. However, it is very difficult to keep up with this type of maintenance, and the best bet may be contacting the supplier and ordering a new tank to be installed in your bathroom. Nevertheless, keeping some epoxy resin on hand for emergencies is a good idea.

If you have an underground leak in your pipes, it is possible to detect the leak before digging. Today's leak detection equipment is very sophisticated and modern, allowing technicians to detect and pinpoint exactly where leaks are before they go about trying to fix them with professional grade equipment for you.

If water is flowing out from where your meter is located, a professional is required to come out and fix the leak. If your water bill goes up, this is most likely because the leak is on the house side of the water meter. You will need to get a professional to come out and fix the leak.

If the water pressure on your street exceeds 60 pounds, you many want to consider installing a pressure reducing valve. Too much water pressure is actually harmful to your plumbing system and could cause excess water pressure. A pressure reducing valve cuts down your water pressure by almost 50 percent.

To better the efficiency of the water heater, see what size a tank your household requires. If you know how many people are in the home and how many appliances use hot water, you will have a good idea of what size tank is appropriate.

To lessen the amount of hair going into your home plumbing, thoroughly brush hair and use a body brush to remove loose body hair before entering the shower or bath. If it's been a while since you have shaved your legs or face, use an electric razor to remove the longer hair, before shaving in the sink or shower.

When it comes to plumbing, there is never an unsolvable problem. If you feel yourself becoming frustrated with the project, you should try to take a break from what you are working on. The greatest mistakes start to happen when you become angry and inpatient, so take a break and walk outside.

To avoid plumbing disasters in your kitchen, never place hard-to-grind, stringy, fibrous waste, such as poultry skins, banana peels, carrots, celery, or cantaloupe pulp, into the garbage disposer. The disposer can't sufficiently grind these food products and they will clog your sink drain. You should also run cold water down the drain for about 15 seconds before and after using the garbage disposer to flush the waste down the main drain.

Tank-less water heaters are a great space saving alternative to traditional tank units. They are available in many models, some for indoors and some models are capable for outdoor mounting. Tank-less water heaters are known as great money savers when it comes to your water bill.

Make sure that you avoid throwing fats down the drain after you clean up your meal. Fats can solidify over time which can cause a drainage problem and corrupt your water flow. Throw out fats and different types of cooking oils in the garbage after you finish with your meal.

Look closely at your toilets several times throughout the year. Check to see if there are any leaks that you may not have noticed; you can do this by placing five or six drops of food coloring in the tank. If there is a leak, the color will seep into the bowl within half an hour. This process will help you catch a small problem before it gets too out of control.

To avoid having your outdoor faucets freeze up in the winter, detach all hoses before the first freeze. Also, close the shutoff valve that leads to the outdoor faucets, then turn on the outdoor faucets to let any remaining water in the lines drain. Once temperatures warm up in the spring, you can reverse the process.

If you aren't having any luck using a plunger on a clogged toilet, you may want to try pouring warm water into it from waist high. Do this as often as necessary if the water level dips back down again.

If you are using a slower head, see to it that you replace it with one that has good quality. Many times, people think it is okay to buy the cheapest shower head that they can find. The problem with this is that they are not very sturdy and can break much easier.

Many people deal with clogged toilets. However, if your toilet will not flush every time, the water rises to the top, and there is bubbling effect occasionally, this can be due to a much deeper blockage in the main pipe. The main pipe must then be cleaned in order for your toilet to work properly.

You can remove unsightly mineral buildup from your shower head by soaking it in vinegar overnight. This loosens the deposits, and in the morning you only need to wipe off the residue with a rag. If your shower head is high up and not removable, place vinegar in a plastic bag, slip the bag over the shower head and hold in place with a twist tie.

Be sure that the dryer's lint trap is clean. This can save you a lot of trouble, including preventing fires. Search the lint trap to see if there are any tears or holes, this helps to prevent lint from getting into the pipes, which can cause clogs and many other problems.

Never pour grease down the kitchen-sink drain. This will help you avoid clogs in your kitchen sink. Place grease in a can or other receptacles and dispose of in the trash. Grease that has congealed on pots and pans can be wiped off with paper towels that can be thrown in the trash.

To make sure there is no accident or sudden rush of water when you tackle a plumbing project, make sure you are ready for a cleanup. If you go into the work with a huge stack of towels and blankets ready to absorb water, the prospect of needing to actually do it will keep you alert enough to avoid triggering the accident in the first place.

Make sure that the temperature of your home's water heater is not above 120F. On older water heaters, be sure it is not above medium settings. When temperatures get higher than 120, scalding can occur. Also, having the settings above 120F, tends to use more energy than lower temperatures do.

If you are thinking about becoming a plumber

yourself, then you should first try to start out as an apprentice. If you can find a good mentor then you will learn a great deal more from watching and assisting him than you possibly could learn by working on projects alone.

To check for toilet leaks, especially if it seems like your toilet is chronically running, use a few drops of food coloring in the toilet tank. If water is leaking into the bowl, you will see color in about a half hour. Replacing tank parts can repair leaks and greatly save on water consumption.

Tank-less water heaters are a great space saving alternative to traditional tank units. They are available in many models, some for indoors and some models are capable for outdoor mounting. Tank-less water heaters are known as great money savers when it comes to your water bill.

You should never dump grease, fat, or cooking oil down the drain. These fats and oils could solidify in cold pipes and clog your sink. Instead you should put the fats and oils in a dish and wait for it to solidify, then throw it away for garbage men to pick it up.

When using a kitchen garbage disposal, let the water

run for a few minutes even after you shut off the disposal itself. The ground up waste matter generated by the disposal exits your house plumbing via water force and without that water, it can sit in pipes and cause clogs.

To keep your drains moving freely and free from gunk and buildup, pour a half cup of baking soda followed by a cup of white vinegar down each drain once a month. The foaming action helps to push stuck substances through the pipe, while the vinegar neutralizes odors. You can follow this solution with a kettle of boiling water for extra cleaning power.

To conserve hot water each day, run your dishwasher late at night. This will help to maintain an adequate water level for your guests and for your chores in the morning or afternoon. Also, you can increase the supply of water available to you for cooking meals throughout the day.

Ensure that everyone in your household knows how to turn off the main water supply, or knows how to contact someone who can. In the event of a burst pipe or other water-related emergency, you should immediately turn off the water to prevent flooding, structural damage, and a sky-high water bill.

Make sure overflow holes are cleaned out. This can help to prevent any water damage. Overflow holes are a way to stop water from overflowing if a sink is left on by accident. If the overflow hole is clogged it will not be able to do its job.

While it may seem like a seemingly harmless thing to do, never run potato peels through your garbage disposal. The chemical make up of this seemingly harmless food allows the potato to turn into a thick, viscous substance that can wreak havoc on the disposal itself, with the potential to render it completely useless.

In cold climate areas, sometimes the pipes in the plumbing system freeze. You can thaw them out without calling a plumber. Before beginning this process, open the faucet and begin thawing closest to the faucet and then move down the line as sections thaw out. One method you can use is to wrap the pipe with a heavy towel or burlap and then pour hot water over it, set a bucket underneath to catch the water.

Do not be surprised if a plumber charges you more than you expected. Many customers think that fixing a toilet or other drainage problem should be easy, therefore the price should be low. You must remember that not only does a plumber have to charge for labor, but they have to charge for parts that you need.

Correct low water pressure problems caused by sediment buildup by cleaning the aerator. The aerator should be removed and taken apart. Then, clean with a tiny brush swabbed in vinegar. Then all you need to do is rinse and reassemble the aerator before putting it back on the faucet. That should help raise water pressure, as any aerator obstacles will be gone.

Cover pipes that are outside or in cool areas. Use heat tape to make sure that the pipes are completely covered and insulated. This will prevent frozen pipes in the winter, which can be an expensive problem. Check outdoor pipes for other problems such as leaks and cracks which are better to catch early.

Regular maintenance of your plumbing lines is a great idea. Your options are getting your lines snaked or jetted. Jetted is a technology that is proven more effective than snaking is. It gets deeper and cleans harder. So jetting is a good idea next time you are having maintenance performed on your lines.

Check your toilet for any leaks. To find out if your toilet is leaking the only thing you need to do is place a few drops of food coloring in the tank of your toilet. Keep your eye on the toilet bowl; if you notice colored water, you can safely assume that you are dealing with a leak.

One of the ways that you can improve the functionality of your shower head is to clean the mineral deposits from the surface. Unscrew your shower head and soak it in vinegar overnight. In the morning, brush off the deposits with a toothbrush to help the flow of water for your showers.

Protect you plumbing pipes! If you live in an area which has cold winters and are leaving your home for an extended amount of time, protect your plumbing while you are gone! Shut off the main water valve! Drain the system of water by opening the faucets at the highest and lowest points of the house. Also, make sure that you have left some heat on in the house! Set the thermostat to at least 55 degrees Fahrenheit.

If you have a leak and your water bill is going up,

there is a method you can try before you call a professional. You can use the red-dye system to detect whether the leak is above ground, underground, or whether it has anything to do with the toilets.

Never try to undertake a project that you are unsure of. Additionally, never call on a friend to help you with something, if they are not a professional. There have been hundreds of good friendships ruined by a guy claiming to know exactly what he is doing, when the truth is he is clueless.

Clean washing machine lint traps and use pantyhose over the water outlet tube to prevent lint, fuzz and other debris from clogging sewer or septic system filters. Fine mesh traps are also available for this purpose, but a package of knee-high nylon stockings and plastic ties can provide enough filters to encourage you to do the job regularly.

To clear mineral deposits from your showerhead, try a soak in white vinegar. Simply add a cup or two of vinegar to a plastic bag and tape it around the showerhead, ensuring that it is submerged. Leave the bag on for an hour, and the vinegar will dissolve the mineral build-up, allowing water to gush through like it was when it was new.

To conserve hot water each day, run your dishwasher late at night. This will help to maintain an adequate water level for your guests and for your chores in the morning or afternoon. Also, you can increase the supply of water available to you for cooking meals throughout the day.

Before starting any plumbing project be sure to turn off the main water supply. Water damage can be one of the most expensive things to repair. To minimize damage turn the main water supply off as well as any shut off valves near where you are working. This will save a great deal of hardship later on.

Use the sounds you hear from your pipes to help you to determine what they problem is. Certain sounds mean the water pressure is too high. Other sounds can signify loose pipes or slight clogs from calcium or iron build up. Listening to your pipes can save you a lot of money hunting down the problem.

To prevent frozen pipes, always keep the living spaces in your house above freezing, even if you aren't home. Any exposed pipes need to be insulated against the outdoor temperatures. But, be advised that your pipes may freeze if the surrounding temperature near those pipes is less than freezing. In the best case scenario, you will have to wait until they thaw so that the water runs again. But, they could also burst, causing a mess and a large repair bill.

Drain the sediment from the bottom of your hot water heater twice a year to keep the hot water heater working at its optimal levels. Simply open the drain valve and allow the water to run out into a bucket until the water runs clear. Then close the drain valve.

In cold climate areas, sometimes the pipes in the plumbing system freeze. You can thaw them out without calling a plumber. Before beginning this process, open the faucet and begin thawing closest to the faucet and then move down the line as sections thaw out. One method you can use is to wrap the pipe with a heavy towel or burlap and then pour hot water over it, set a bucket underneath to catch the water.

The key towards maintaining low plumbing repair bills is prevention. Drain clogs are probably the most frequent issue you will run into with your plumbing. Drains are easily clogged by hair. Putting a strainer on your drain can solve this problem. Taking the hair off of the screen and disposing of it is cheaper and easier than removing it from the pipes.

Do not be surprised if a plumber charges you more than you expected. Many customers think that fixing a toilet or other drainage problem should be easy, therefore the price should be low. You must remember that not only does a plumber have to charge for labor, but they have to charge for parts that you need.

Frozen pipes can lead to many problems, most of them expensive to fix. So you want to avoid that at all costs. To avoid frozen pipes, make sure the temperature in your home never drops below 55 degrees. Look for any air leaks around your pipes and make sure they're sealed up.

In any DIY plumbing project, make sure that you always test the drains and the supply lines before you close up the walls. It is a lot easier to find and solve problems if you look for them while you are still in the process of actively doing the job.

One of the ways that you can improve the functionality of your shower head is to clean the mineral deposits from the surface. Unscrew your shower head and soak it in vinegar overnight. In the morning, brush off the deposits with a toothbrush to help the flow of water for your showers.

When looking for a plumber, you have quite a few options. Ask friends for recommendations of who they use. Check online for plumbers with good reviews and references. Use your yellow pages and look under "Plumbing Contractors" or "Plumbing, Drain and Sewer Cleaning". Make sure that you contact more than one plumber before making a choice.

Education is essential when dealing with plumbing issues, because knowing nothing about the topic will cause people to spend big bucks on a plumber. If you own your own home, it's important that you take the time to learn the basics of plumbing, enough to ensure that you know what a plumber will be doing. This helps prevent them from ripping you off.

To prevent the most common kitchen sink clogs, avoid putting any sort of solid foods down your drain. Many foods, such as eggs and vegetable and fruit waste actually harden with exposure to cold water and over time can form clogs that are next to impossible to remove without professional help.

If you cannot turn off your main water valve before leaving on vacation, turn off the individual valves for the toilets, sinks, and washing machine. If the valves do not look like they are in good working order, then leave them on and that will be something that you need to have changed when you return.

If you think you understand what is wrong with your toilet, but aren't sure, you should first do some more research on the internet. Most plumbing problems are fairly standard, and you should be able to read about the problem in great detail on several amateur plumber forums to make sure you understand the problem.

Plumbing choices can come in many ways. One decision you need to make as a homeowner is to purchase a tank-less water heater. One thing to remember if you are considering a tank-less heater. You will pay two to three times more than if you purchase a tank heater.

If you are paying someone else to do the plumbing in your home be sure that they are licensed in your state to do that work. Some people who have little or no knowledge of plumbing will try to pass themselves off as a pro. So you can see the importance of checking to see if your plumber is licensed. You should also see if you can find positive testimonials about the plumbers work.

Before starting any plumbing project on your own be sure to do a great deal of research. There are many resources available to assist you in understanding your plumbing system and help you to avoid many common mistakes made by do-it-yourself novices. Reading about other people's mistakes can make the difference of saving or losing money.

As the weather begins to get cold, attend to all of your exposed pipes by adding insulation to them. Pay particular attention to pipes located in crawl spaces and the outside walls of your residence. Taking this step will help ensure that your pipes continue to function throughout the winter.

If you have issues with the plumbing making a hammering sound when you turn it off, check your water pressure. Any time your water pressure is above 80 PSI, you will hear extra water noise. This can be easily solved by the installation of a pressure-reducing valve, which can be done by most homeowners.

Avoid the bursting of pipes due to the change in the temperature. You need to allow the flow of heat to reach under the sinks and into the pipes, you have to keep the cabinet doors of the bathrooms and kitchens open. It is important to keep water running at both hot and cold faucets along with vanities that are in close proximity to exterior walls.

During the winter, preventing frozen pipes when you live in a small dwelling can be something good to know. Frozen pipes will not only stop your flow of water but can crack and damage pipes. By running a little water out of every faucet during the coldest parts of the day, you can avoid this.

There are many ways to unclog a drain. You can try plunging it at first. If that doesn't work try using a chemical agent from the store. Before you go and spend money at the store though, if you have baking soda and some vinegar handy, you can mix those together and pour them in the drain and try to plunge that but if all else fails they have stronger remedies at your local hardware store.

Make sure everyone in your home knows where the main water shut off valve is and that they know how to work it. That way, if there is a water problem, anyone in your household can turn off the water, thereby reducing the chances that your home will incur major water damage.

Watch how your toilets are flushing. If you have to jiggle the handle or if it takes too long, you might have to repair some toilet parts. Replacing these parts early may help you to save on your water bills and will save you from more expensive repairs at a later date.

One of the things that you can do to maximize the security of your home is to seal all of the cracks in your outdoor faucets. Even a tiny crack can intensify as the season progresses and lead to serious problems down the road. Reduce drips and leaks for optimal protection.

If your plumbing is making strange noises you may have lost something called your "air cushion". To turn this back on, you're going to need to turn off your main water supply. Run all faucets in your house and then turn back on your main water supply. This should make everything sound better again.

DIY plumbing jobs will require that you understand how to solder copper for the lines for the water supply. You can practice this skill so that you will be able to run your lines without worrying about it leaking. Search online for video tutorials that can help you get a handle on how to go about soldering.

If you have clogged pipes, try cleaning them with an enzyme pipe cleaner. Enzyme based cleaners work by using natural bacteria that turns the sludge clogged in your pipes into a liquid, allowing it to flow down the drain with ease. Cleaners containing enzymes are some of the best you can buy.

If you are using PEX tubing for the supply lines in your home, make sure you get the right tools for the job. PEX tubing requires a completely different tool type than regular lines. PEX has a lot of benefits though, so don't let the different requirements throw you off.

If your toilet is constantly developing moisture on the outside, you may want to consider turning up the heat in your bathroom. The biggest cause of "sweaty" toilets is cool and moist air. Believe it or not, this moisture could actually cause damage to your toilet, so it is crucial that you fix the problem.

Have your pipes in your plumbing system frozen? You can skip the cost of hiring a plumber by using this method. First, open the faucet so steam produced by the thawing process can escape. Begin thawing close to the faucet, and move down the line as each section thaws out. Use a hair dryer or a heat lamp to warm along the pipe. Even though this method consumes quite a bit of time, it is safer than most other heating methods. Furthermore, it requires no cleanup.

If your pipes bang when you turn on the water, and all the pipes are anchored correctly, you should add some straps or cushion the pipes with a rubber blanket. There may be times when you will need to do both. Make sure that if you have copper pipes, you are not using galvanized straps.

When starting a plumbing project that is due to loud noises in your pipes empty the pipes first. This can be an easy fix to an otherwise wasted huge job. Just close the main water line and open the facets throughout the house. After the water has stopped flowing turn the water on from the main source and check to see if the noise is eliminated.

If your toilet is slow to flush, add some white vinegar to the overflow tube. White vinegar helps the water from your tank to flow quickly, which will make the toilet flush faster. It is recommended that you use about a quart of the vinegar and let it stay there for at least an hour before flushing.

You should avoid using blue toilet tablets, bleach tablets or any other odor removers in your toilet. These products can be great when it comes to getting rid of odors, but unfortunately, they can cause significant damage to the rubber portions of your toilet. This can lead to it breaking down or having other issues.

During the winter, preventing frozen pipes when you live in a small dwelling can be something good to know. Frozen pipes will not only stop your flow of water but can crack and damage pipes. By running a little water out of every faucet during the coldest parts of the day, you can avoid this.

Set the temperature on your hot water heater to a temperature that does not exceed 120 degrees. This helps to save energy and prevents the water from becoming too hot and potentially scalding someone in your household. Older models that do not have a temperature setting should be set on Medium.

Basic problems with toilets can be a quick fix for even the rawest amateur plumber and is worth attempting if you can take the time to research the problem. Seek out the necessary part or parts from your local hardware store and ask for support in how to properly install them.

If you need to buy a pipe cleaner to unclog your pipes, it is best to find one that is enzyme based. The natural enzymes in these cleaners dissolve the clog, turning it into liquid, freeing it from the pipes. Enzyme cleaners should be your first choice.

Make sure that your tool box is ready for any project you are preparing to do. The last thing you want is to be knee deep in a job only to find that you are missing the one tool you need to finish. Be sure to have various sizes of pipe wrenches that can be used to complete any job.

Never pour grease down the kitchen-sink drain. This will help you avoid clogs in your kitchen sink. Place grease in a can or other receptacles and dispose of in the trash. Grease that has congealed on pots, and pans can be wiped off with paper towels that can be thrown in the trash.

Keep an eye on the hoses for your dishwasher and washing machine. These hoses can leak and bulge, which can be a problem. Check them for signs of wear and tear and replace any hoses more than 10 years old. You'll find that these hoses age well, but you have got to make sure they are doing the job they should.

Cover pipes that are outside or in cool areas. Use heat tape to make sure that the pipes are completely covered and insulated. This will prevent frozen pipes in the winter, which can be an expensive problem. Check outdoor pipes for other problems such as leaks and cracks which are better to catch early.

One way to prevent water heater problems is to turn down the heat. As long as the water is still as hot as needed for showers and washing dishes, turning it down won't hurt anything, and will extend the life of the heater. Holding very hot water can corrode the inside.

Have a specific plumber in mind before you have an emergency. Most people don't think about plumbers until they find themselves having a big problem that needs to be fixed right away. Instead, choose a plumber who you are comfortable with and whose experience you trust--way before you actually need his services.

Make sure that the temperature of your home's water heater is not above 120F. On older water heaters, be sure it is not above medium settings. When temperatures get higher than 120, scalding can occur. Also, having the settings above 120F, tends to use more energy than lower temperatures do.

For people who live in an apartment complex, plumbing is often forgotten about. The first time they move into a home they are unable to resolve any minor plumbing problems, because they have never dealt with this kind of thing. It is good to get a basic understanding when moving into your first house.

When facing temperatures below freezing in the winter it is important to leave the hot water dripping. This makes sure that the pipes don't freeze over and saves you the expensive repair of fixing and or entirely replacing a broken pipe. The slight cost of dripping hot water is well worth saving you from that large expense of replacing a broken pipe.

If you are paying someone else to do the plumbing in your home be sure that they are licensed in your state to do that work. Some people who have little or no knowledge of plumbing will try to pass themselves off as a pro. So you can see the importance of checking to see if your plumber is licensed. You should also see if you can find positive testimonials about the plumbers work.

It is important to know how to properly anchor your pipes when it comes to plumbing. This is extremely important to know because not having your pipes well anchored could result in loud noises, leaks, or pressure problems. Call a professional if you are unsure how to take care of it yourself.

If your toilet is slow to flush, add some white vinegar to the overflow tube. White vinegar helps the water from your tank to flow quickly, which will make the toilet flush faster. It is recommended that you use about a quart of the vinegar and let it stay there for at least an hour before flushing.

Unclog drains with ease. Try using a plunger and drain cleaner, as your clog may simply be a build-up of hair and debris. If this doesn't work you may have to clear the drain with a snake. Feed the snake into the drain line as far as it will go. Turn the crank gently, which will help to loosen the clog. Remove the snake, and run water down the drain to see if the clog has been removed. You may have to use the snake a couple of times, before the clog is cleared so don't give up!

Periodically check your pipes for leaks and cracks. These can be forgotten, since pipes are usually hidden away, but checking for leaks and cracks can help you identify a small problem before a big problem occurs. You may have to enlist the help of a family member to turn on and off the water stream as you are checking.

At least once a year remove the faucet aerator and clean the screens. This helps it properly function. The function of a faucet aerator is to allow for an even flow of water and to conserve water. Be sure to clean out the aerator and you'll notice a these things working.

Make sure everyone in your home knows where the

main water shut off valve is and that they know how to work it. That way, if there is a water problem, anyone in your household can turn off the water, thereby reducing the chances that your home will incur major water damage.

If the hot water heater in your house is over ten years old, you should look at replacing it. Hot water heaters are very susceptible to corrosion on the bottom. This can lead to leaking and flooding whatever room it is in. Then not only will you have to replace it, but you'll have to fix any damage caused by the leak.

When getting an estimate from a contractor on a job, make sure to ask how long the written estimate is good for. For big jobs you usually want to get estimates from a few different plumbers. Knowing how long your estimate is valid will help you know what your time limit is for making a decision on whom to hire.

Make sure your plumbing contractor has the proper insurance before letting them work in your home. This is a big problem with all types of construction contractors. They may have the proper licenses, but because of the high cost of insurance, they may not be properly insured and can end up on your homeowner's policy if they get hurt.

Make sure that the temperature of your home's water heater is not above 120F. On older water heaters, be sure it is not above medium settings. When temperatures get higher than 120, scalding can occur. Also, having the settings above 120F, tends to use more energy than lower temperatures do.

Watch out for decreased levels of intensity in the water flow in your bathroom. This can be a sign of calcium or mineral deposits disrupting water flow. If spotted early enough it may be possible to remedy this without having to replace the pipes.

If you are going to update the plumbing in your house, one thing to consider is installing a new tank-less water heater. They are much smaller than traditional tank heaters, which is a space-saver. Tank-less water heaters are available in gas or electric, depending on what your house needs.

Having to wiggle the toilet handle or hold it down to get your toilet to fully flush indicates that the tank parts need to be replaced. Kits that include all of the parts needed can be purchased in any hardware or home improvement store to easily do the repair yourself.

When working outside, it is important that you take regular breaks to give yourself some relief from the sun. Wrapped up in complicated work, you forget the danger of sun exposure over a long period of time.

To help keep your drains working properly you should pay attention to clogs. Clogs are a common problem at home but with proper maintenance and preventive measures you can avoid a messy situation. Clogs are not only an annoyance, but can also lead to overflows and water damage. So make sure you keep your drains clog-free by implementing easy preventative practices.

Make sure you know where your home's water shutoff is located. You never know when there might be an emergency involving a broken pipe or damaged connection that requires you to turn off the water right away. In addition, knowing where the shutoff is located is vital before you start any plumbing project, in case anything goes wrong.

Ensure that everyone in your household knows how to turn off the main water supply, or knows how to contact someone who can. In the event of a burst pipe or other water-related emergency, you should immediately turn off the water to prevent flooding, structural damage, and a sky-high water bill.

Do not fall for the idea that liquid grease can be easily washed down the drain with hot water. While the grease may flow past the initial drain with the water, it does not take much of a temperature change as it moves through your pipes to alter from liquid to solid. The repeat habit of dumping grease in the sink is a sure-fire way to ensure a hard-to-reach clog forming in the future.

If you have a clogged drain, don't use cleaning chemicals to try to clear the clog. These harsh chemicals can corrode your metal pipes leading to leaks and broken pipes over time. Instead, stick to a plunger or make use of a plumbing snake to clear them.

Check your gas water heater periodically to make sure the pilot flame is lit. The correct color for this flame should be blue. The tip of the flame should be yellow. If you find that you are only seeing a yellow flame, you may need to call a professional for safety reasons.

Your water heater works more during the fall and winter so make sure that you eliminate all sediment buildup around this piece of equipment. Flushing this device can lead to increased longevity so that you do not face plumbing problems during the winter. This precaution will save time, money and effort.

Frozen pipes can lead to many problems, most of them expensive to fix. So you want to avoid that at all costs. To avoid frozen pipes, make sure the temperature in your home never drops below 55 degrees. Look for any air leaks around your pipes and make sure they're sealed up.

If you have sewage backing up into your toilet, this is due to a blockage in the branch line connecting the main line and sewage line. You can run a device through this called a snake to try to clean up the clog. Or you can also purchase some specific drain cleaner and hope that works. If not, you'll have to call in the professionals.

The valves that are hardly ever used have their way of somehow fusing together. You have to turn them often to avoid sticking, and keep penetrating them with oil.

The Department of Consumer Affairs is a great place to check if you need a plumbing contractor. You will be able to check their license and know if people have complained about this specific contractor. A contractor's license must be in good standing and current for you to even consider him.

Teach your children how to notice plumbing problems. Many parents handle plumbing issues without sharing that information with their children, who grow up not knowing anything about plumbing. Any time you make a small repair or notice a problem, call your kids in and explain what the problem is and what you are going to do. Educate them so they can make good decisions in the future.

Be sure to have a running toilet fixed as soon as you can. Having a running toilet uses more water, which raises your water bill. To fix it yourself, you just have to find out what the problem is and buy the supplies you need. If you can't fix it yourself, call a plumber.

You should consider getting a stainless steel sink if you are in need of a new sink. Stainless steel sinks are much better than other ones for many reasons.

They are more durable, they absorb shock, they are easier to clean, and they go with almost any decor.

If your water bill seems unusually high and you haven't changed your water usage, the problem is most likely in the service line. The cost to hire a professional to find and repair the service line most often is far greater than installing a new line and then having the old one shut off permanently.

Always try plunging any clogged toilet or drain before snaking. Snaking can often push problems further down the pipe and make matters worse. A plunger uses nothing but your strength and water pressure to help clear clogs. For more effective plunging, boil some water and pour into the affected drain or toilet to help loosen things up before plunging.

Before starting a plumbing project be sure to know your pipes. Each pipe has a different use and every municipality has different codes for what pipes can be used for. Making a mistake in this area can be very costly, if you are forced to remove all the pipes from the work you have just completed.

If you are starting a plumbing project due to a leak be sure to tighten all the nuts first. Loose areas are the number one cause for leaks. If after tightening all nuts in the area you find that the leak continues, it is then time to search for possible holes.

Do not try to sell a product that you do not agree with. This includes paying attention to the company itself and their values and policies. If you have any qualms about the company, your customers will pick up on it. You want to be a full supporter of the product you are selling

If a pipe ever freezes, you need to make sure to shut off the water. This will keep the pipe from bursting and causing you major damage to your home. Make sure to shut the water off at the main valve, and then open the faucet that is closest to the frozen pipe so it can drain while it is thawing out.

Have a professional flush your septic tank every five years or so to keep it working well. This prevents sediment from building up in the tank and causing a backup into your home or causing the failure of the septic system itself. If the cost of pumping your septic tank seems a bit steep, remember that the cost of cleanup and repair of a failed septic system will be much higher.

If you have issues with the plumbing making a

hammering sound when you turn it off, check your water pressure. Any time your water pressure is above 80 PSI, you will hear extra water noise. This can be easily solved by the installation of a pressure-reducing valve, which can be done by most homeowners.

Certain things shouldn't go into your plumbing system. By knowing what you can and cannot flush or throw into the garbage disposal and sink, you can save yourself from a costly repair or disaster. A plumber can usually get your plumbing back into working condition, but can be avoided if you know how to dispose of items correctly.

If your sewer is backed up, there are things you can do to troubleshoot and clean, including renting equipment like a main line cable. However, often times this does not fully take care of the problem. A professional needs to assess the issue then, using a camera method, and thoroughly cleaning the main line.

If water is flooding your home, immediately switch off the main electrical power. If water comes into contact with any electrical components, it can become a fatal situation. Once the power is off, then deal with the flood water. Put your own and your family's personal safety first, and show each member of the family how to shut off the power.

If you own property where the temperature gets below freezing for an extended amount of time each year, you should make sure that pipes located in unheated areas, such as crawl spaces and garages, are insulated. Pipes that are exposed to the outside elements or those that are prone to freezing, should be protected by heat tape or thermostat-controlled heat cables to prevent them from freezing.

If you are looking into becoming a plumber, there are a few things that you should know first. The most important thing is that plumbers who work for companies do not make a high salary. You should try to find a way to work for yourself, in order to increase your earnings.

To compare the quality of your pipes or sewers over time, create a video for documentation purposes. Several months later, make the same video so that you can see if there are any new cracks or holes that require fixing. This can serve as a great way to analyze your infrastructure.

For homeowners interested in energy-conserving

appliances, you might consider the tankless water heater model. Unlike a conventional water heater, these do not store any water, and heat up the water only as it is needed. You will save some money on your energy bill.

To avoid plumbing disasters in your kitchen, never place hard-to-grind, stringy, fibrous waste, such as poultry skins, banana peels, carrots, celery, or cantaloupe pulp, into the garbage disposer. The disposer can't sufficiently grind these food products and they will clog your sink drain. You should also run cold water down the drain for about 15 seconds before and after using the garbage disposer to flush the waste down the main drain.

Plumbers earn a very good wage, so hiring an apprentice can be a great idea. Not only is this a good way to have cheap labor, it is also very fulfilling to pass on what you know to a younger person.

Is your shower pressure weak due to clogging of the openings in your shower head? Here is a simple and cost-effective tip t

o take care of that problem. Pour a cup of vinegar into a plastic bag, place it over the shower head, and twist tie it into place so it can soak overnight. In the morning, remove the plastic bag and use an old toothbrush to scrub off the mineral deposits which are clogging the openings. This will help to restore water flow and increase shower pressure.

Avoid plumbing problems! Do not stop up the toilet! Some common items that will stop up a toilet include: toys, hair, paper towels, birth control items, and feminine personal products. Do not flush these items down your toilet - unless the instructions say otherwise! These can stop up your toilet - to the point that nothing else will work - except calling a plumber!

Rigid copper is used for main water lines in many homes. You cannot bend rigid copper, so joints and tees must be soldered on. When soldering, always apply flux (also called soldering paste) to both surfaces. Flux retards oxidation when the copper is heated. Always use lead-free or nearly lead-free solder when sweating a copper joint.

Before you start a plumbing project you should tighten all of the pipes that are easily accessible. Especially if your pipes are making a range of loud banging sounds, as this is a clear sign that there are loose pipes along the line. It is also a good idea in case there is a clog so the excess pressure released does not break a loose pipe.

Make sure you know where your home's water shutoff is located. You never know when there might be an emergency involving a broken pipe or damaged connection that requires you to turn off the water right away. In addition, knowing where the shutoff is located is vital before you start any plumbing project, in case anything goes wrong.

If you have noisy pipes, you can cushion them with a rubber blanket or add additional anchor straps. Banging pipes are usually caused by loose pipes, water hammering to a stop as you turn it off, or hot water pipes shifting in their position. All of these problems can be solved by cushioning and anchoring the pipes.

Make sure overflow holes are cleaned out. This can help to prevent any water damage. Overflow holes are a way to stop water from overflowing if a sink is left on by accident. If the overflow hole is clogged it will not be able to do its job.

During the winter, preventing frozen pipes when you live in a small dwelling can be something good to know. Frozen pipes will not only stop your flow of water but can crack and damage pipes. By running a little water out of every faucet during the coldest parts of the day, you can avoid this.

Find out the plumbing codes in your local area before starting any project. Plumbing codes can vary wildly from area to area and you don't want to run afoul of the codes. Visit your local building department to find out information or hire a plumber for a day to help you go over your plans and provide advice.

Your water heater works more during the fall and winter so make sure that you eliminate all sediment buildup around this piece of equipment. Flushing this device can lead to increased longevity so that you do not face plumbing problems during the winter. This precaution will save time, money and effort.

The best way to avoid plumbing bills is to prevent problems before they happen. Drain clogs are probably the most frequent issue you will run into with your plumbing. You can clog your drains with hair. Screens and drain covers are great ways to stop hair from going down your drains. Cleaning hair from the screen is a much easier affair than it would be to get the hair out of the pipe.

Make sure to pour a gallon or two of water into drains that are used infrequently. Not only does this make sure that they are clear when you need them, but can also fill the trap and make sure that unpleasant odors don't enter your home. Doing this periodically will also help you to catch problems before they become serious.

Do not forget to check the temperature of the water heater in your house, especially if you are planning to leave for an extended period of time. You should keep the temperature no higher than 120 degrees, which will help to reduce energy use and prevent your system from burning out.

Periodically, make sure that the sump pump in your house is working to full capacity. Pour a few gallons of water into the sump pit, and your pump should drain that water out with minimal issues. Checking that your devices are working throughout the year can pay large dividends in the event of a crisis.

Ask before the plumber comes out if they charge for the consultation. In order to quote a project, the plumber has to come out to inspect your particular issue. It is standard to charge for the consultation appointment but the prices can vary wildly. Ask upfront so that you aren't surprised by the total.

When plunging a drain to attempt to remove a blockage, first make sure that the drain is completely covered in water. This helps to form a seal. Then, plunge at least fifteen to twenty times before stopping. Repeat the process two to three times. If this doesn't work, try a chemical drain cleaner.

Teach your children how to notice plumbing problems. Many parents handle plumbing issues without sharing that information with their children, who grow up not knowing anything about plumbing. Any time you make a small repair or notice a problem, call your kids in and explain what the problem is and what you are going to do. Educate them so they can make good decisions in the future.

Do not give a plumber the entire payment for a job until the whole job is completed. You may have to pay a portion of the cost before the plumber works on the job, but you should never have to pay in full until after everything has been correctly finished.

Agree with the plumber in advance on the job and payment.

It is important to know how to properly anchor your pipes when it comes to plumbing. This is extremely important to know because not having your pipes well anchored could result in loud noises, leaks, or pressure problems. Call a professional if you are unsure how to take care of it yourself.

To avoid having your outdoor faucets freeze up in the winter, detach all hoses before the first freeze. Also, close the shutoff valve that leads to the outdoor faucets, then turn on the outdoor faucets to let any remaining water in the lines drain. Once temperatures warm up in the spring, you can reverse the process.

Making sure you know all of your problems so you can have them fixed by one plumber visit is very beneficial. Having them all fixed in one visit takes a lot of money off of your bill because you don't have to pay for the visit multiple times so make sure you make a list first.

It is not always necessary to call in a plumber when you have a damaged section of pipe in your plumbing. There are repair kits you can buy in your local hardware store which are excellent in repairing leaks. If you have a small leak, you can rub a compound stick over the hole or crack in the pipe to seal it shut. Epoxy paste is also an excellent remedy for a leaking pipes. Make sure you turn off the water and completely dry the pipe before applying the epoxy.

If water is not coming to the dishwasher, you most likely have a blockage somewhere. You will need to turn off the water supply and remove the hose that leads to the dishwasher. After securing the hose, turn the water back on. See if it feeds into a bowl. If not, then you must find the block where it is at which may include removing more piping.

Have you tried patching your pipe with the store-bought patching kits only to have that section of your plumbing continue leaking? Replacing the damaged pipe is a more permanent solution than patching. First, you must shut off the main water valve, and drain the water from the damaged section. Cut out the damaged section of the copper pipe, leaving about an inch of extra pipe on both sides of the damaged area. Remove corrosion from inside the pipes with a wire brush. Apply flux to the replacement pipe and the remaining pipe. Slide the piece of replacement pipe into place with couplings. Apply solder all around the joint, and use a propane torch to solder the replacement section into place.

To avoid sediment buildup, drain gallons of water from your water heater to flush any corrosion. This will help your heater to run more efficiently therefore saving you regular energy costs. Make sure to read your heater's instructions before attempting this, and do this periodically to make sure that your heater is running as well as it can.

If you are using a slower head, see to it that you replace it with one that has good quality. People will buy the cheapest option thinking it will do the job they need it to do. The problem with doing that is the cheaper shower heads are not known to be sturdy, and they tend to break easier.

Before embarking on a plumbing project, make sure that you're aware of where the shutoff valve for water in your home is, as well as the valves for shutting off individual structures like sinks, toilets, etc. This way, if something goes wrong, you'll be able to stop the water flow.

Garbage disposals are a common cause of plumbing

problems, which is an easy problem to solve. Don't just put everything down the disposal or treat it like a second trash can. Use the disposal things that would be difficult to dispose of normally. Putting all leftover food down the sink is a good way to produce clogs.

Sometimes kitchen sinks can be clogged up due to a slow accumulation of solidified grease. One quick fix for this is to try pouring very hot grease down the sink, which will liquefy the grease clogging the drain and carry it down. Water won't work, because grease will not dissolve in water.

While it is possible to do plumbing activities yourself, it is generally not recommended. If you are not sure of what you are doing, then you must hire a professional. This will help to insure you don't make a bigger mess of the small problem that your plumbing previously had.

Be sure that you check on your water meter when it is not being used. Then, check on the meter 8 hours later. If the meter has changed, even a small amount, this could be a sign that there is an undetected water leak, which can be a severe problem.

* * *